THE PROUDEST HORSE
ON THE PRAIRIE

THE PROUDEST HORSE ON THE PRAIRIE

by Beatrice S. Smith
illustrated by Laurel Horvat

Published by
Lerner Publications Company
Minneapolis, Minnesota

International Standard Book Number: 0-8225-0702-1
Library of Congress Catalog Card Number: 74-128804
Second Printing 1972

About 60 years ago, along the Little Missouri River
in South Dakota, a colt was foaled. He was broad shoul-
dered and well formed, with wide-set eyes and deeply
arched ears. His coat was a gleaming rust, and his tail,
mane, and lower legs were a rich black.

His ancestors were fine domesticated animals. His
dam was a very sensible mare, although she did not
like to be ridden. Unfortunately, she died when the little
colt was barely able to stand. But in just a few days he
was running with another dam and her colt. Finding a
foster mother was not difficult for an intelligent horse
like this one.

The early years of his life were gay and carefree. His playground was the Elmer Wickham ranch, which stretched across the prairie as far as one could see. In the range country of this untamed land, colts were allowed to run free for three or four years before they were gentled.

A few people believe that if the orphan had been handled at an earlier age, his life would have turned out differently. Others disagree; they say this particular horse had the look of an eagle from the day he was born. On one point everyone agrees: this certainly was no ordinary colt.

Unlike most horses, he had an outstanding sense of smell. He could detect a small pool of water from a great distance. At the scent of a stranger he rolled his eyes and flattened his ears against his head.

His sense of taste was also well developed. He especially liked fruit, and once he was seen trying to climb an apple tree.

His eyesight was so good that one of his owners swore the horse could see behind him. This animal allowed no one who was wearing spurs or carrying a stick to come within 20 yards of his hindquarters.

Nor did he like to be touched.

He had excellent hearing, as most horses do. Sudden noises set his nerves on edge. In fact, he was so sensitive to sound that he flicked his ears when phonograph records were played inside a farmhouse half a mile away.

He also had a *sixth* sense, and that was what made him most unusual. For example, he loved the excitement of a storm and always seemed to know when one was coming. Elmer Wickham used to predict the weather by how wildly the gelding galloped around the pasture.

The horse had a sense of fun too. When he first saw snow, for example, he frolicked like a young child. He put his head down and ran in circles, first one way, then another. He dragged his nose through the snow, rolled in it, and even ate it.

He also enjoyed playing games. His favorite play-
mate was a big German shepherd dog. On one day the
dog, nipping and yipping, would chase the horse. On
the next day the horse, rearing and kicking, would chase
the dog. How the two managed not to hurt each other
was a mystery to everyone.

    Another playmate was a mule named Molly. A pack animal, Molly had an unusual fox-trot gait that helped her move easily without rocking her load. Somehow the gelding picked up the same gait, and the two animals were often seen ambling side by side across the prairie. There was no fence or gate or door that they could not figure out how to get through. If all other methods failed, the gelding simply picked up his right hoof and broke down whatever was blocking the way.

When it came time to train the horse, Elmer chose Fred Wheat for the job.

"Watch out, Fred. That bay is a wild one," Elmer warned.

"Don't worry. I can handle him," Fred replied. He approached the gelding carefully, however. He knew that horses differ not only in color and size but also in personality, just as people do. Also, there was an expression in the young bay's eyes that made Fred a little nervous. But he was sure that he would have no real trouble.

Like all trainers, Fred Wheat had his own method for breaking and starting young colts. He believed that one of the most important lessons any horse had to learn was how to stand still. When he trained a horse, Fred simply hobbled the animal's front legs, placed a halter on him, and tied him to a solid fence until he became quiet.

This horse, however, would have none of that. When Fred hobbled *his* front legs, the strong young bay reared and kicked until he fell to the ground. He lay there only long enough to regain his strength. Then he leaped up and bucked and thrashed some more.

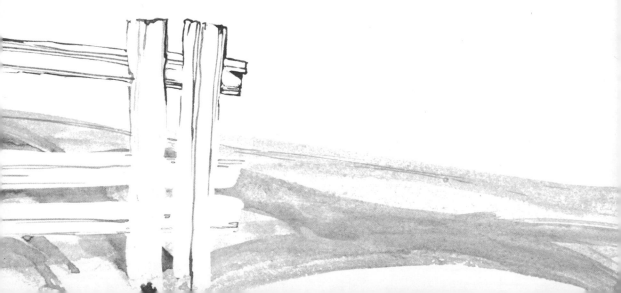

"Easy, boy, easy!" Fred kept shouting. The words did not help. Nothing helped.

The only method left was to hobble the horse's hind feet and sideline them to his hobbled front legs. Even this arrangement did not tame the spirited bay.

"Every day it is like meeting a moving locomotive head on," Fred complained. After months of trying and failing, Fred finally gave up.

By this time the horse was a full-grown bay gelding, darker than most, but very handsome. However, no matter how handsome he is, an unbroken gelding is of little use on a ranch. When he learned that Fred had given up, Elmer Wickham sold the horse.

The young bay changed hands many times in his early years, living first in one home, then in another. He was treated roughly by several owners, and he carried scars that proved it. One owner crosstied him and beat him with a knotted rope. Another blindfolded him and ran him into a solid wall. After going through these experiences, the gelding did not have much trust in human beings.

When World War I began, the armies in Europe needed horses for their cavalry divisions. Buyers from as far away as England, France, and Italy came regularly to the small range towns in the United States to purchase horses. The young bay, who now belonged to a man named Doc Latham, caught everyone's eye because he was so strong and handsome. He appeared to be an outstanding cavalry horse.

But cavalry horses had to be ridden, and anyone who dared to mount this animal was in danger of being thrown to the ground and slashed by flying hooves.

"He's too mean to handle," one French army officer said. The other buyers quickly agreed.

Doc Latham was so upset that he sold his horse to two businessmen he happened to meet on the street. The price was only five dollars.

The new owners did not know much about horses, so they hired Ed Marty, a well-known cowboy, to try his hand at saddling the spirited animal.

Ed had been around horses all his life. When he was a young boy, he worked for several cattle outfits in the Dakotas. Along with his other chores, Ed was given the job of breaking colts. After a time he developed an ability to ride bucking horses. Naturally, he was certain that he knew exactly how to handle this one. No horse had ever got the best of him.

Lightly flicking his long whip, Ed moved the horse into the corner of a small corral. Then he slipped a halter on him. Next he attached crossties from either side of the halter to the top rail of the corral fence. After he finished crosstying the horse, Ed fastened a heavy knotted rope to the long black tail. The rope would hit the bay sharply when he kicked up his hind legs. To keep the horse from throwing his head back, Ed attached a leather strap, a "tie-down," to the underside of the noseband. Finally, Ed blindfolded the high-strung animal, so that he would not "spook."

Now that the horse could not see or buck or rear or roll, Ed was able to slip a saddle on his back and mount. By this time a large group of people had gathered around the corral. No one spoke. Almost everyone in the crowd seemed to be holding his breath.

"Ed's done it. The big bay isn't so tough after all. Why, he doesn't look as if he could buck off a wet saddle blanket," Ed's friends whispered to each other.

What they said seemed to be true. The horse was standing very still. He did not move even after Ed's friends unfastened the crosstie.

"Walk!" Ed leaned forward and gave the command sharply.

The gelding refused, and Ed did what any cowboy would have done. He gave the horse a sharp dig with his spurs. That was his downfall.

Old-timers say that the dust has not settled yet. The angry horse unwound like a coiled spring and thrust the surprised cowboy high in the air. Ed landed flat on his back in the mud. The horse leaped over the fence and headed for the cactus flats.

As the gelding ran off, Ed sat up slowly and looked after him. Then he grinned and sang out, "It's a long, long way to Tipperary," a line from a popular song of the day.

"Hooray for Tipperary!" a small boy shouted.

"Tipperary! Tipperary! Hooray for Tipperary!" the spectators cheered.

In his short lifetime the proud horse had been given many names by many people, but this was the first appropriate one. However, no one could call the horse by his new name because he had disappeared.

Flying dust and a barking dog indicated the direction that Tipperary had taken. Ed and his friends were about to run him down, but at that moment something unexpected happened.

A team of horses, startled by the runaway animal, pulled loose from their hitching post and dashed down the street at a full gallop. Their rig lurched behind, its rear wheels skidding from side to side.

Every dog, as well as every man and boy, ran after the team. Merchants who had goods on display in front of their stores shouted and waved their aprons to scare off the approaching runaways. Girls screamed. Babies cried. The team plunged on, even more frightened by the commotion they were causing. However, when the horses tried to go around either side of a flag pole, they were abruptly stopped by the yoke that linked them together. Luckily, no one was hurt and nothing was broken. But the event was important enough that it caused Tipperary to be completely forgotten until he was far away.

There are many tales about what happened to Tipperary during the next few months. Some people say that he joined a band of wild mustangs. Others believe that he made friends with a dusky-maned wolf. Still others say that he was captured by a tribe of Indians. One story is especially interesting: according to Mrs. Rose Schilling, Tipperary became the trusted pet of her 12-year-old son Louis.

Louis Schilling was blind. One day he discovered Tipperary in a wooded path near his home, Mrs. Schilling said. At first Louis thought that he had found Goldie, his own mare, who sometimes managed to escape from the corral. So Louis ran his hands over the horse, from head to tail, to "see" if he had been injured. In doing this, of course, Louis discovered that the powerful bay was not Goldie. Talking softly, he continued to pet and quiet the animal.

"The horse was damp with sweat and breathing hard, so I knew he'd come a long way," Louis later told his mother. "Since he was not wearing a bridle or a halter, I couldn't lead him home. All I could do was leave him there and notify the sheriff."

The next morning, certain that the horse would be far away, Louis went about his regular chores. He noticed that Goldie seemed a little restless, but he thought nothing of it, because mares are often restless.

At noon the runaway appeared. Mrs. Schilling spotted him on the far side of the corral. He was stretching his neck over the fence to drink water from Goldie's tank.

"I'd better catch him and put him in the corral," Louis told his mother.

"Louis had been riding anything with four legs since he was two years old, so I wasn't afraid for him," Mrs. Schilling reported.

Whether Tipperary sensed that the young boy was blind or whether the bay was tired of running is impossible to say. But he stood quietly while Louis slipped a halter on him, and then he allowed himself to be led into the stable. There Louis rubbed him down, combed his mane and tail, and gave him a pail of oats.

Thinking that soon someone would come for the gelding, Louis continued to care for him. Three weeks passed in this manner. Finally one morning the boy decided to saddle up the big horse, "just to see what he could do."

"He swung his hindquarters just once, that was all," Louis told his mother. "And he laid his ears back when I mounted him. I talked to him, and after a minute or two he relaxed and off we went."

"There seemed to be a complete understanding between my son and that horse," Mrs. Schilling said. "Louis would decide what direction they would take. Then when he thought it was time to go home, he would give Tipperary his head and they'd come back."

Mrs. Schilling continued, "The only time Tipperary refused to let Louis mount was a day in early September. Three hours later a tornado swept through the area. It passed not two miles from our place."

When asked why she felt so sure that this runaway was the bad-tempered Tipperary, Mrs. Schilling replied, "I'm not. But Louis is, and that's enough for me."

Perhaps Louis Schilling was right. There are one-man (or one-boy or one-girl) horses just as there are one-man dogs. It is possible that Tipperary had finally found his "man." But why did the horse break away and leave Louis after a short time?

"He wanted excitement. It was too tame around here for him," Louis claimed. Perhaps. It is also possible that Mrs. Schilling and her son were mistaken. No one will ever know for sure.

Whatever the case, one winter day a South Dakota rancher named Charlie Wilson caught sight of the big bay on the southern tip of his land, near the state line. Like most ranchers, Charlie knew a good horse when he saw one. Uncoiling the rope from his saddle horn, he measured the distance carefully. Then he flung the lariat with all his strength.

The noose flew high and caught. One sharp twitch and Charlie had captured a horse. Snorting and screaming, the great animal struggled to free himself. He could not. The rope was strong and so was Charlie Wilson.

The rancher sensed trouble, however. Usually an untamed horse, once he is captured, follows willingly when tied to a steady mount's saddle horn. Not this one. He bucked every mile of the way back and once nearly unseated Charlie from his horse.

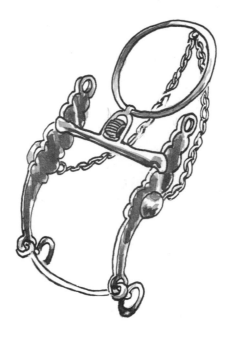

Since only the most skillful cowboys worked at Charlie's ranch, he was certain that his men could easily handle the roughneck. He was wrong. The experts tried every trick they knew, but the horse refused to settle down.

"He's loco, that's what," one cowboy complained.

"No," Charlie said. "I believe we're using the wrong bit. Every horse is different," he explained. "Every mouth is different, every head length, every jaw width. Every tongue has a different thickness. You have to find a bit that will make the horse comfortable. Then he will be happy in the mouth. And when he's happy in the mouth, he's happy in the mind, and he'll work for you."

Although the cowboys were not convinced, they experimented with several different bits. One they tried was an old-fashioned Spanish ring bit which had copper rollers to keep the horse's mouth moist. For a minute it looked as if this one might work. But only for a minute. Then Tipperary threw his head in the air, rolled in the dirt, kicked, and screamed.

"What that horse needs is a good whipping. He's like a kid with a tantrum," one cowhand remarked.

Charlie shook his head. "He's already been whipped too much. Look at the marks on him."

"We could try blowing on his nose. The gypsies say that's the best way to make a horse feel friendly," another hand suggested, half seriously.

"I'd try it, if I didn't think I'd get my head chewed off," Charlie replied, staring gloomily at the horse. Suddenly he snapped his fingers. "Gentleness! Maybe that *is* the answer. We'll start handling him as if he were a newborn foal. Though why I bother, I don't know."

So began weeks of patient handling. Every day Tipperary's trainers petted him, scratched his back, gave him treats. Soon the big gelding stopped running every time someone came up to him. Then a halter with a soft sheepskin cover was slipped over his head, and he wore it for a few minutes each day. Next a long lead rope was attached to the halter, and the trainers led Tipperary to his dinner, a pail of oats flavored with sugar and salt.

Then Charlie himself drove the horse on foot, teaching him to respond to rein signals from behind. After that, he was exercised on a longe rein, a special training rein. Then he was given the Spanish ring bit that he had found comfortable. The final step was to have him become accustomed to wearing a saddle. First he carried a blanket. Then he carried a saddle, then a sandbag tied to the saddle.

Now Tipperary supposedly was ready to be ridden. He had been very cooperative and had done everything well. Yes, he should have been ready.

He wasn't.

The instant a cowhand threw his leg across the saddle, the gelding bucked the man off. Once the horse went so far as to rear up and strike a fallen rider. He would allow no one on his back, not even Charlie. And that was that.

"You devil!" Charlie shouted. But he said to his men, "You know, I can't help admiring that horse. Nobody is going to make a slave out of him. I don't know when I've felt so challenged by an animal."

"I doubt there's a man alive who can stay on him for more than a second or two," one cowboy commented.

"I'd like to see some smart aleck try," another said.

"So would I," agreed Charlie, grinning. It was then that an idea struck him. Many people would enjoy seeing this proud horse perform. There was only one place where Tipperary could be useful and happy—the rodeo.

The only sports contest native to the United States, the rodeo developed in the early frontier days. It originated with the roping and riding contests the Western cowboys held for their own amusement. As local champions began to challenge champions from other ranges, the contests attracted spectators. After a few years, rodeos were organized regularly, as they continue to be today. A rodeo has several scheduled events, including bull riding, steer wrestling, calf roping, and bronc riding.

In a bronc-riding contest a cowboy climbs into a chute and eases down on the back of the horse whose name he has drawn. A moment later the chute gate flies open. A blur of bucking horse and jerking rider streaks across the arena. The ride is supposed to last eight seconds.

The horse does everything he can to unload the rider. But the rider is under several limitations: he can use only one hand to hold on to the reins, and he is not allowed to change hands, let go of the reins, or lose the stirrups. Nor is he permitted to touch the horse or gear with his free hand. The longer a cowboy stays on, and the rougher the ride, the higher the score.

Two officials stand in the arena to judge the contestants. A total of 100 points is possible for each ride, but any score over 65 is considered above average.

The purpose of the bronc-riding competition is simply to settle the old question: which cowboy is the best rider? Untamed, spirited horses are needed for the test.

"Certainly Tipperary will offer a ride that is difficult enough to satisfy anybody," Charlie told his cowhands. As for deciding which cowboys were the best riders, he was sure that this horse had his own ideas about that.

Charlie put Tipperary into a string of bucking broncs and started going to rodeos. In his first rodeo, Tipperary came out of the chute twice. The first time, he bucked off an up-and-coming young cowboy in two seconds flat. His second victim was an older fellow who had a reputation for being able to ride horses other men found impossible. Tipperary dumped him in four seconds.

At the end of the show, the big gelding was voted best of all the broncs present. Everyone was impressed. Tipperary was entered in several more rodeos, and almost overnight he became a star. The song "Tipperary" was played each time he dashed out of the chute. Tail swishing, ears lying flat, eyes rolling white, the horse would plunge to the center of the ring and grind cowboy after cowboy into the dust.

It was not long before many contestants refused to ride the famous horse when they drew his name. Special prize money was offered to any rider who dared to try. Only the truly professional riders had enough courage.

Sam Brownell, a world-champion rodeo cowboy, was one of the few men who managed to stay on Tipperary for more than three or four seconds.

"It was just luck," Sam said at the time. "Tipperary had me unseated in the first couple of jumps. But he changed directions as I was going off, and I landed in the saddle again."

Many great riders had a chance on Tipperary's back, but the untamable outlaw went after every would-be rider as if he intended to remove all cowboys from the face of the earth. And they loved him for it. A high jumper and kicker, Tipperary also was the kind of bronc that the rodeo judges liked. The audiences loved him because he put on such a good show.

Tipperary seemed to enjoy the sport as much as the contestants and spectators did, and he did not suffer any ill effects from his work. Although he bucked over a thousand cowboys off his back in nearly 20 years, he remained perfectly sound to the end.

Finally, in 1926, Tipperary's owners wisely decided to retire him to the green pastures he had known as a colt. But a year later, by popular demand, he was called back for another performance at the rodeo in Belle Fourche, South Dakota. He had helped make that rodeo one of the most famous in the country.

When it was time for his appearance, Tipperary
was led into the arena. He was older now and seemed
changed: he looked slow, gentle, tame, easily handled.
The spectators grew silent. Was this horse their hero?
No, he couldn't be.

Then the band struck up "Tipperary." That was the
old champion's cue. He threw up his head and jerked
away from his trainer. He flattened his ears, humped
his back, and reared and bucked in front of the excited
crowd.

Everyone in the audience stood up and began to cheer. The clapping and shouting lasted for nearly an hour. One old-timer got so excited that he jumped off the top of the bleachers, a distance of 20 feet.

It was Tipperary's last public appearance.

In February of 1932 a blizzard hit the Dakota prairie. Somehow Tipperary found a way out of the stable. He had always loved storms, but this one proved to be too much for him.

The great horse was not forgotten after he died, however. People continued to talk about his courage and his independent spirit. Twenty-three years after Tipperary's death, a monument was dedicated to him in a Buffalo, South Dakota, roadside park.

It is standing there today for all to see. The words on the monument are:

WORLD'S GREATEST BUCKING HORSE
TIPPERARY
1910 — 1932

The Author

Beatrice S. Smith is the author of numerous articles and short stories for both adults and children. Her work has appeared in such publications as the *NEA Journal, Grade Teacher, Junior Life, Christian Home, Venture,* and many others. A graduate of the University of Wisconsin, Mrs. Smith has taught English in California, Wisconsin, and Brazil. *The Proudest Horse on the Prairie* is her first published book. Mrs. Smith lives in Middleton, Wisconsin, and she also has a farm in the central part of the state. She has spent much of her life around horses, and her household includes her husband, two sons, two horses, a cat, and a dog.

The Artist

Laurel Horvat is a graduate of the Minneapolis School of Art and has a Bachelor of Fine Arts degree in graphic design. As part of her studies, she spent a year at the Gerrit Rietveld Academie in Amsterdam. Formerly employed by the Augsburg Publishing House and by the Hallmark Company, Mrs. Horvat is now a freelance illustrator and designer. She especially enjoyed her work for *The Proudest Horse on the Prairie* because she is an avid horsewoman as well as an artist. Another book illustrated by Mrs. Horvat is *Lancelot the Ocelot*. The artist and her husband reside in Providence, Rhode Island.